C000242712

TOGETHER
AND FAITH?

SHOULD THE CHURCH BLESS
SAME-SEX PARTNERSHIPS?
A RESPONSE TO THE BISHOP OF OXFORD

VAUGHAN ROBERTS

The Latimer Trust

Together in Love and Faith? Should the Church bless
same -sex partnerships? A Response to the Bishop of Oxford
© Vaughan Roberts 2022. All rights reserved.
ISBN 978-1-906327-78-1
Cover image: Canva
Published by the Latimer Trust, 2022.

Scripture quotations are taken from the Holy Bible, New International
Version®, NIV® Copyright ©1973, 1978, 1984, 2011 by Biblica,
Inc.® Used by permission. All rights reserved worldwide.

The Latimer Trust (formerly Latimer House, Oxford) is a conservative
Evangelical research organisation within the Church of England, whose
main aim is to promote the history and theology of Anglicanism as
understood by those in the Reformed tradition. Interested readers are
welcome to consult its website for further details of its many activities.

The Latimer Trust
London N14 4PS UK
Registered Charity: 1084337
Company Number: 4104465
Web: www.latimertrust.org
E-mail: administrator@latimertrust.org

*Views expressed in works published by The Latimer Trust are those of
the authors and do not necessarily represent the official position of The
Latimer Trust.*

CONTENTS

Introduction

In his essay, *Together in Love and Faith*, Bishop Steven Croft explains how he came to change his mind concerning committed same-sex partnerships and argues that they should now be fully recognised and celebrated by the Church.[1] He also proposes a settlement, which would provide for differentiation of provision and oversight for those who could not support this change. Given that he makes it clear that he writes self-consciously as a bishop, his arguments will no doubt receive careful attention, not least in his own diocese. As an incumbent in Oxford, I feel a sense of responsibility to explain why I, along with many others in the diocese, do not agree with him that the Church should change its position on this matter. I do, however, believe that elements of the second part of his proposal offer a hopeful basis for a potential way forward for the Church of England out of the present unsatisfactory situation.

When, over twenty years ago, the then Bishop of Oxford, Richard Harries, gathered his clergy for a discussion about issues relating to sexuality, he began by urging us to engage with those with whom we disagree at their best. Bishop Richard always modelled that himself, and I honour Bishop Steven for always seeking to do the same. He has been consistently kind and respectful, as demonstrated, for example, by his sharing his essay

---

[1] Steven Croft, *Together in Love and Faith: Personal Reflections and Next Steps for the Church* (Oxford, 2022).

with me and inviting comments before publication. I, in turn, extended the same courtesy to him. As will be clear, there is much we disagree about, but we are united in recognising the integrity of the other, as one who is seeking to be faithful to Christ. This is a debate between Christians and we have both sought to engage in it Christianly. That is what I understand to be 'good disagreement', even if the differences go very deep and are found in the end to be irreconcilable.

Some background

Bishop Steven begins by describing something of his 'own story and journey'. Perhaps it will help give some context to what follows if I do the same.

I was raised in a nominally Anglican family, but found Christianity irrelevant and dull until I read Matthew's Gospel in my last few months at school. I had not been searching, so it was a surprise to find myself confronted by the beauty and arresting power of Christ's life and teaching. Somehow I knew that my life could never be the same again and, after a brief period of private struggle, I began to follow him. I knew instinctively that coming to Christ involved repentance: not just turning to him, but also turning away from old ways of thinking and living. That was not easy, not least relationally, as some friends could not accept the change in me, but the Spirit had given me a deep awareness of Christ's lordship and his love for me and I wanted to please him in all areas of life, whatever the cost, and that included my sexuality.

As a young Christian, I understood, both from my own reading of the Bible and from teaching I received, that the place for sex was in heterosexual marriage. That was challenging for all of my new Christian friends, but I sensed there was likely to be a greater cost for me, given that I found it hard to imagine ever being married to a woman. I had experienced some attraction to girls, but that had largely faded by the time of my conversion and was soon to disappear completely. I am grateful that I was taught at that time about the goodness, not just of marriage, but also of singleness, whether chosen or not. There have certainly been some very hard times in the years since, but I have never regretted my decision to follow Christ. The joys of Christian discipleship have far outweighed the sorrows and, as many discover, the greatest joys have often come in and through the greatest struggles, including for me in the area of sexuality.

I began by reading law at Cambridge, but switched to theology with a view to future ordination, having already attended a ministerial selection conference. After a brief period as assistant to the Anglican Chaplain at the University of the Witwatersrand in Johannesburg, I came to Wycliffe Hall in Oxford and have been in the city ever since. I was ordained by Bishop Richard Harries in 1991 and was at first curate at St Ebbe's, before being appointed Rector in 1998.

Although I have stayed in the same place during those 30 years, the surrounding culture has certainly not stood still, not least in matters relating to sexuality. In

1991 the notorious Clause 28, introduced by Margaret Thatcher's government, which prohibited the 'promotion of homosexuality' by local authorities, was firmly in place, the age of consent for homosexual acts between men was 21 and civil partnerships, let alone same-sex marriages, were unthinkable to most people. The changes since then, both in legislation and in public attitudes to homosexuality, have been dramatic and have led, understandably, to increasing calls, from without and within, for the Church of England to catch up with society and change its own teaching and practice.

The resulting debates within the Church, which have often been very heated, have been a cause of anguish for me. I have never wanted to be any kind of campaigning controversialist, having a deep dislike of conflict and a longing just to focus on the work I love as pastor of a local church, with occasional forays for evangelism and Bible exposition elsewhere. Furthermore, the issues under discussion are deeply personal for me and there is a heavy emotional cost in engaging with them, especially in conflictual settings, as I know there is for many others on both sides of the issue.

All the discussion has, of course, made me think. Through much reading and in long conversations I have engaged with many people, who hold very different perspectives to mine. I have learnt much from them and have been moved by the accounts of their experiences, including at times, very sadly, testimonies of unquestionably bad treatment from conservative Christians, whether from ignorance or worse. Change has certainly been needed, both in attitudes and pastoral practice. I myself have benefited from changes that have already taken place, but the process is not complete. And yet, for reasons I will outline later in this paper, I remain persuaded by the truth and goodness of the traditional Christian understanding that the right place for sex is only within heterosexual marriage and that any change to that position should be resisted as being unfaithful to God and harmful in its effects.

Very little of my ministry has been focused on matters relating to homosexuality. I have only spoken specifically on the subject in more detail a handful of times at St Ebbe's, and then almost always in the context of a wider treatment of sexual ethics. My strong preference has been to avoid public engagement on the matter, but there have been times when I have felt in conscience that I must not be silent. In so doing, I have always wanted to stress that the issues involved are not only theological or political, but deeply personal and pastoral. I have been especially conscious of the impact of these public debates on gay/same-sex attracted Christians in our churches and it was largely with them in mind that I decided to be open about my own sexuality. I was delayed by the caution of some friends, but finally did so in 2012 in an article in *Evangelicals Now*.[2] At the time, there were few public examples of same-sex attracted Christians, who

---

[2] Vaughan Roberts, 'A Battle I Face', *Evangelicals Now*, October 2012.

held to traditional views on sex and marriage, and I knew of no other pastors. I am glad to say that the situation is very different now.

Part One: Should the Church
bless same-sex partnerships?

Listening to the pain

In describing his own change of view, and in advocating a change in the Church of England's position, Bishop Steven focuses on three arguments: from experience, culture and Scripture. Experience comes first, with an account of the distress caused to many because of the Church's current attitudes to sexuality. This distress certainly needs to be recognised, heard and, as far as possible, felt.

A sense of alienation has long been a part of the experience of sexual minorities. As someone who grew to adulthood in the 1980s, at a time when homophobic attitudes were widespread and largely unchallenged, I know something of that at first hand. I picked up sufficient warning bells to give me an instinctive sense that it was not safe to be open with others. The resulting silence about my sexuality added significantly to the sense of isolation I already felt because of the realisation that I was different from my friends. In reality, I received a wonderfully warm reaction whenever I did pluck up the courage to speak, but the general atmosphere, both in the wider world and in the Church, made me very cautious about doing so.

If I were a young adult today, my experience would be very different. The general mood in the culture, with significant exceptions of course, is one of understanding and affirmation towards those who do not fit the sexual 'norm'; in fact there is a widespread rejection of any sense that there is such a norm. Diversity is celebrated and openness encouraged. This can have a negative impact, with some young people being encouraged to adopt a label too quickly, at an age when they may well experience significant confusion, not least in the area of sexuality, but there are real benefits. Many, who would previously have experienced their sexuality as a cause of isolation and shame, can now feel a much deeper sense of being known and accepted. These gains, in Bishop Steven's account, serve to magnify the contrast felt by LGBTQ+ Christians between the affirmation of the world and what they experience from the Church, in ways that can cause 'acute pain and alienation from the community in which they might be entitled most to expect love, understanding, acceptance and respect'.[3]

The first response to this claim needs to be a humble, contrite recognition of the truth that churches have often been at fault and caused harm through our attitudes and actions. Those of us who hold to a traditional position on sexuality can be quick to reject criticisms of such behaviour by claiming they are exaggerated and present a false picture. There may be truth in that, but we must not hide from the reality that, even if the worst excesses

[3] Croft, *Together in Love and Faith*, 13.

are rare, prejudice, ignorance and insensitivity remain and can cause some to feel that they are unlovable and unwelcome, even if that is often far from the intention.

I should say at this point that my own experience has been almost entirely positive in recent years. Some had warned me about speaking openly about my sexuality, fearing that it would negatively impact my ministry but, almost without exception, that has not been the case. The initial reaction was full of love, acceptance and affirmation, after which, to my great relief, almost everyone continued to relate to me exactly as before, albeit with a greater understanding of one aspect of my reality.

In contrast with the welcome I received from traditional Christians, the reaction from progressives was often ambivalent and sometimes hostile, including from some gay advocates for change. There are those who find it uncomfortable to be reminded that the LGBTQ+ community, including those who are Christian, does not speak with one voice, or have one experience. It is, in my view, a weakness of Bishop Steven's essay that he does not give sufficient weight to this reality. There is a reference to one meeting with some same-sex attracted Christians, who hold to the traditional teaching of the Church, but there is no evidence of any greater engagement with what is a significant group. There is no reference, for example, to the ministry of Living Out[4] and True Freedom Trust[5]

[4] www.livingout.org.
[5] www.truefreedomtrust.co.uk.

or of powerful testimonies, such as David Bennett's in his book *A War of Loves*, which includes deep theological reflection.[6] It feels as if Bishop Steven is engaging with the evangelicalism of 20 or 30 years ago, when, by his own admission, he had hardly begun to hear the experience of LGBTQ+ people himself. We have all been on a journey since then, including those of us who have not changed our minds about the Bible's teaching on sex and marriage.

The most powerful and prophetic critique of prevailing conservative attitudes towards sexuality that I have read comes, not from outside that tribe, but from within, in Ed Shaw's *The Plausibility Problem*, which upholds the traditional view, but contains many challenges to the evangelical culture.[7] We still undoubtedly have a long way to go, but there have been significant changes. There are many same-sex attracted Christians who, like me, are grateful for the love, companionship and support we receive from our Christian friends and local churches, as we seek to live a faithful life of discipleship in the face of the bemusement and sometimes open hostility we receive, not just in the world but, it has to be said, increasingly from the wider Church. Same-sex attracted Christians who hold to the traditional teaching on sexuality are in the uncomfortable position of being

---

[6] David Bennett, *A War of Loves: The Unexpected Story of a Gay Activist Finding Jesus* (Grand Rapids: Zondervan, 2018).

[7] Ed Shaw, *The Plausibility Problem: The Church and Same Sex Attraction* (Nottingham: IVP, 2015).

a minority within a minority within a minority. Some have spoken out publicly, but most are largely hidden. The deep pain they feel at being undermined by church leaders who are, in effect, telling them that their efforts to remain godly are unnecessary, needs to be recognised, along with any wider engagement with the experience of LGBTQ+ people in our churches.

Observing the fruit

Alongside listening to the pain of LGBTQ+ Christians, the other argument from experience to which Bishop Steven appeals is an observation of fruit: both the positive fruit he sees in faithful same-sex relationships, as well as the negative fruit he believes is produced by the Church's traditional teaching.

There is no doubt that there are many, and increasing, examples of long-term same-sex relationships, which exhibit admirable qualities. That does not mean, however, that the relationships are morally good in every aspect, or that the positive fruit is necessarily a result of them being sexual. Are not the same qualities also evident in many committed celibate friendships? In my early years in ministry I witnessed a number of examples of two people of the same sex, usually women, sharing a home and, to a significant extent, their lives. Together they provided support for one another and much blessing to others. I fear that such arrangements are less common now, because of an assumption in our overly-sexualised world that such a relationship must be sexual.

In describing the negative fruit of traditional teaching, Bishop Steven seems close to accepting the assumption of many in our contemporary culture that normal people cannot live healthy, happy lives without sexual intimacy. This means, in his portrayal, a range of unattractive alternatives for all but the few gay/same-sex attracted Christians who are able to embrace and live out a call to celibacy: marriage to someone of the opposite sex, a double life, or reluctant and miserable singleness. There are no doubt many who do fit within his categories, but there is a serious lack of nuance in his analysis of this fruit, which is too negative in its portrayal of celibacy and singleness.

Both the Lord Jesus and the Apostle Paul spoke positively about singleness, whether deliberately chosen 'for the sake of the Kingdom of heaven' or as a result of other factors (Matthew 19:10–12; 1 Corinthians 7:32–35). As I think of the older saints whose example and love have most impacted my life, all of them experienced great challenges and a disproportionate number were single, some, I imagine, because of same-sex attraction, although I am not aware of them having ever spoken publicly about that. Only the Lord Jesus knows exactly what lay behind the beautiful fruit they exhibited of love, contentment, joy and compassion, as well as a manifest intimacy in their relationship with him, but I have no doubt that in every case the gold came out of the furnace of suffering. This is not a theology of masochism. There is no merit given in Scripture to those who choose pain for the sake of it, but when accepted and embraced with and for Christ, the resulting fruit is beautiful. I have seen that fruit in the lives of many faithful same-sex attracted celibate people.

Let me stress again that I in no way minimise the pain of unchosen celibacy. In my own way, and everyone's way is different, I have experienced that myself, alongside many blessings. Christians have often magnified the pain by teaching higher standards of sexual morality, while doing little or nothing to foster the friendships and community which make such a lifestyle liveable. Faithfulness may require celibacy, but it certainly does not demand a life of isolation. We need to work much harder to build churches which help develop relationships of deep intimacy with Christ and with one another. That will be a blessing to all and especially to those who are single, whether because of their sexuality or the many other reasons why Christians find themselves unmarried.

Responding to cultural shifts

There is no doubt that the cultural changes over the last few decades in relation to sexuality have resulted in significant dislocation between Church and society. Whereas not long ago a traditional Christian approach to sexuality was widely affirmed, even if it was less commonly practised, it is now often regarded as harmful and even immoral. Those who seek to uphold orthodoxy in these matters in the Church are regarded as heretics in the world, in resisting values and beliefs that, it is assumed by many, should be upheld by all right-thinking people.

Bishop Steven is certainly right in recognising the missional challenge caused by these cultural shifts, but there is, of course, nothing new in the Church experiencing such dissonance within and hostility from its surrounding culture. In fact the Lord Jesus told his disciples to expect no less: 'You do not belong to the world, but I have chosen you out of the world. That is why the world hates you' (John 15:19). In the history of the global Church down the ages a gap between it and the society it inhabits has been normal. In such circumstances, the question which arises is whether that gap can and should be reduced by wise cultural adaptation for the sake of mission ('To the Jews I became like a Jew, to win the Jews', 1 Corinthians 9:20), or whether such changes should be resisted out of faithfulness to the apostolic faith. Before making that decision we need, I suggest, to look more deeply at what lies behind our culture's assumptions and their wider consequences.

A celibate same-sex attracted pastor friend of mine always seeks to broaden the issue when challenged about his views concerning homosexual behaviour. He says: 'Before I answer, you need to understand that we probably have a radically different view from one another, not just on this issue, but about the whole purpose and meaning of life.' That recognition is a helpful starting point, but it is lacking in Bishop Steven's essay. Describing how, especially for a younger generation, the Church's traditional position on sexuality is seen to fall short of their deeply felt standards of justice and fairness, he comments: 'we are seen to inhabit a different moral universe'.[8] He is right about that, but he fails to engage with the reality that the difference goes way beyond contrasting approaches to one issue alone, but is the result of a completely different mindset about the whole of life, which is manifest in the sexual revolution of the last few decades. It is important to recognise both the roots of that revolution, as well as its fruits.

Beginning with roots, the difference between the moral instincts of contemporary society and the traditional teaching of the Church flows from two different worldviews, both of which could be called gospels, because each claims to present good news which offers an alternative path to freedom and fulfilment. The gospel of 'expressive individualism', to use the sociologist Charles Taylor's term, prizes authenticity as its core value. Jonathan Grant has expressed it well:

> Modern authenticity encourages us to create our own beliefs and morality, the only rule being that they must resonate with who we feel we *really* are. The worst thing we can do is to conform to some moral code that is imposed on us from outside – by society, our parents, the church, or whoever else. It is deemed to

---

[8] Croft, *Together in Love and Faith*, 20.

be self-evident that any such imposition
would undermine our unique identity.[9]

This way of thinking is in the cultural air we breathe:
in advertising slogans ('Be whatever you want to be' –
PlayStation), movies (it's the moral to almost every fairy
story, once it has received the Disney treatment) and in
the lyrics of our favourite songs ('Look out 'cos here I
come. And I am marching to the beat I drum... This is
brave, this is bold, this is who I am meant to be. This is
me' – *The Greatest Showman*).

It all sounds intoxicating, and we sing along with the
songs with gusto, but behind the message is a profound
individualism, which resists any restrictions to the self's
right to self-define and to live accordingly, including
those previously understood to be imposed by biology
and nature. The old binary categories of straight and
gay, and even male and female, are now increasingly
rejected in favour of a growing suite of identity labels and
associated lifestyles. In repeated surveys more than half
of young adults are resisting the categories of gay and
straight and place themselves somewhere on a spectrum,
with increasing numbers defining themselves through
terms such as omnisexual or polyamorous. We would
be naive to think that moral instincts shaped within this
world of expressive individualism would be satisfied if

---

[9] Jonathan Grant, *Divine Sex: A Compelling Vision for Christian
Relationships in a Hypersexualised Age* (Grand Rapids: Brazos
Press, 2015).

the Church just adapts its position in relation to same-sex unions alone.

Along with its roots, we should consider the fruit of the sexual revolution. There have certainly been many gains, not least in freeing people from some of the overly-oppressive social conventions of the past. Women, perhaps especially, have benefited, for example, from easy access to effective contraception and a stress on the importance of consent for sex, as well as the promotion of sexual pleasure for both sexes, not just men. But there has been much bad fruit as well. The prioritising of self-fulfilment above obligation, and feelings above commitment, has led to the collapse of the family unit, bringing devastating consequences for the whole of society, felt disproportionately by children, women and the vulnerable. Instead of bringing freedom and fulfilment, the legacy of the revolution for many individuals has been isolation and insecurity. This is evident especially among young people, who are facing epidemic levels of anxiety. This is hardly surprising, given that they are now being expected to decide, not only what subjects to take for exams, but to define their gender and sexuality at an age when hormones are raging and much feels uncertain.

Nowhere in his essay does Bishop Steven grapple with these wider aspects of the sexual revolution. His advocacy of 'a modest redrawing of the boundaries of what constitutes... sexual immorality', begs many questions.[10] If we are to feel free to make changes in relation to same-sex unions, on what basis can we resist the calls, which will inevitably come, for further boundary changes? If, in supporting this change, we have rejected an understanding of sexual ethics which has been held by the whole Church down the ages until very recent times, on what basis can we speak with authority into our confused and hurting world about any other aspect of sexual morality? Do we really think that the proposed change will result in large numbers returning to church? The churches that are full of young people tend to hold to traditional teaching, which offers a distinctive message, rather than an echo of what they hear elsewhere.

Surely what is needed in the face of the disjunction between Church and society is not accommodation, but rather a winsome, confident re-presentation of the riches of Christian teaching about sex and marriage. Pope John Paul II has shown us the way in his *Theology of the Body* (1979–84), made accessible in various publications by Christopher West.[11] Jonathan Grant's *Divine Sex* and Glynn Harrison's *A Better Story* are also excellent models of how to present the Bible's vision for sex and sexuality with winsome clarity, while engaging with the realities

---

[10] Croft, *Together in Love and Faith*, 37.

[11] E.g. Christopher West, *Theology of the Body for Beginners: A Basic Introduction to Pope John Paul II's Sexual Revolution* (West Chester, PA: Ascension Press, 2004, 2009).

of the modern world.[12] What we have to offer is not oppressive moral rules, but a God-shaped, gospel-soaked vision for the whole of life, including sexuality, which is certainly challenging, but also gloriously liberating.

The authority of Scripture

Bishop Steven begins his section on Scripture by affirming 'the authority and primacy' of the Bible and stressing that there should be no shortcut in the Church's position on sexuality without serious engagement with its teaching. This is exactly what we would expect from someone from his tradition, but what follows is an essentially liberal, rather than evangelical, approach.

The Bishop gives an indication of his direction of travel when he writes,

> As I listen to the stories and experiences of LGBTQ+ people, all of my pastoral instincts point to finding a way of interpreting the Scriptures that allows for greater love and support, tolerance and the blessing of [same-sex] partnerships, even where this interpretation seems, at first sight, to be in conflict with some of the obvious interpretations of key biblical passages.[13]

---

[12] Glynn Harrison, *A Better Story: God, Sex and Human Flourishing* (London: IVP, 2017).

[13] Croft, *Together in Love and Faith*, 27–28.

The impression is given of a conclusion that has already been made and, given the stated desire to find a way of reading the Bible that supports it, it is no surprise that he is successful in the attempt. This is not a classical Anglican approach to authority in which, while tradition and reason are taken very seriously, they are subservient to Scripture as the supreme authority. Our engagement with experience and culture will raise questions, which we will then rightly bring to our reading of the Bible. At that point an acceptance of the authority of Scripture should allow it to present its own questions and challenges in response. There is little evidence of such dialogue in Bishop Steven's argument, which is not surprising, given the principles he establishes for reading the Bible, which ensure that any such challenges are blunted before they are received. This does nothing to challenge the conviction of many that the argument in relation to same-sex partnerships is more about the authority of Scripture than its interpretation.

Christ at the centre

We can all agree about 'the testimony of Scripture to human equality and worth'.[14] This, I trust, is not in doubt and, whatever our understanding of the Bible's teaching about sexual morality, we are surely united in seeking to treat everyone with respect and dignity.

---

[14] Croft, *Together in Love and Faith*, 26.

It is also common ground that Christ should be at the centre of the way in which we read Scripture, but Bishop Steven's assertion that it therefore follows that we should 'establish the primacy of mercy over judgement' in our reading and application of the Bible is highly contentious.[15] He argues that 'to follow the primacy of mercy means to be willing to change and adapt pastoral practice alongside the culture we seek to serve, as it itself changes in the light of new knowledge and understanding'.[16] A consistent observance of that principle would, of course, require many more changes than just in relation to same-sex unions. Following the way of Christ requires us, he says, 'to prefer and privilege, in our discernment, the way of mercy' when there is a perceived clash between the Church's 'dual vocation to mercy and to holiness'.[17] But is this really the way of Christ? He did indeed condemn the judgementalism of the Pharisees, but he did so while, if anything, reinforcing stronger moral demands than theirs, rather than slackening them (Matthew 5:20). He was certainly merciful to the woman caught in adultery, but he also urged her to 'go and sin no more' (John 8:11). And, most profoundly of all, through the cross he forgives us in ways that satisfy both the Father's mercy and justice (Romans 3:25–26).

There is no doubt that Christians have often been guilty of prioritising judgement over mercy in matters of sexual

---

[15] Croft, *Together in Love and Faith*, 28.

[16] Croft, *Together in Love and Faith*, 28.

[17] Croft, *Together in Love and Faith*, 28.

morality. The correct response to this is not to make the opposite error. The way of Christ involves taking the costly path of upholding both mercy and justice, rather than allowing either to cancel out the other. There is a glorious inclusivity in the gospel: *all* (whatever our sexuality) have sinned and therefore face God's righteous judgement; *all* (whatever our sexual history) are offered God's mercy through Christ by grace; and *all* (whatever the different challenges involved) are called to live a life of repentance and faith.

The silence of Jesus

Is it really correct to say, as Bishop Steven does, that Jesus 'is largely silent on the matters of human sexuality'?[18] It is true he says nothing direct in relation to homosexual behaviour, but he does affirm the teaching of Genesis 2:24, which is the foundation of all the Bible's teaching about sex (e.g. Mark 10:5–9). It was universally accepted by all first-century Jews that sex should not take place outside the marriage of a man and a woman. The only area of debate was over divorce and remarriage, which is why Jesus engages with that subject. There was no need for him to speak about homosexual practice, as none of his audience would have been in any doubt that it was wrong. The argument from Jesus's silence, therefore, works against any change to the Church's practice in this area, rather than for it.

---

[18] Croft, *Together in Love and Faith*, 28.

The Bible's grand narrative

Bishop Steven's engagement with Scripture on the subject of same-sex partnerships is focused on addressing the small number of texts which, he acknowledges, on a surface reading at least, appear to prohibit sexual behaviour between people of the same sex. He is right to acknowledge that these verses have 'down the years been weaponised against LGBTQ+ people in deadly ways', which have caused great pain.[19] Too often they have been taken out of context and used in a manner that has left some same-sex attracted people feeling that they are in a uniquely sinful category. The power of the rhetoric used has at times not been matched by equal force given to condemnation of heterosexual sins, which receive a much greater focus elsewhere in Scripture, or to the wonder and transforming power of God's loving grace towards us all in Christ. A responsible presentation of the Bible's teaching on this subject will not focus simply on a few texts, but will be placed in the context of the grand narrative of the Bible's story. All the Bible's teaching about sex, or indeed any other matter, needs to be understood in the light of the overall story of redemption, which is Scripture's main theme.

The foundation of the Bible's teaching on sex and marriage is found in Genesis 1 and 2. In the first creation account we are told: 'So God created mankind in his own image, in the image of God he created them; male and

---

[19] Croft, *Together in Love and Faith*, 30.

female he created them' (Genesis 1:27). Bishop Steven comments: 'This is a sophisticated account of gender. We are one common humanity before we are gendered beings, male and female. It seems to me this truth is able to accommodate fluidity, minorities and exceptions in our understanding of gender, as part of the wonderful diversity of creation.'[20] This, however, is not the natural reading of the text. There is no suggestion here that primal 'man' was originally androgenous and only later was divided into male and female. In God's design we are created men and women and our sex is fundamental to who we are.

The second account of creation gives us more detail. Adam is created first and then God says 'It is not good for the man to be alone. I will make a helper suitable for him' (Genesis 2:18). The helper God creates is not another man, but a woman. In the words of Thomas Schmidt: 'Adam is not given a mirror-image companion, he is given a *her*, and he delights in her *correspondence* to him (Genesis 2:23), which resides both in her likeness (human) and her difference (female). The pair are literally and figuratively made for each other'.[21]

Having created our complementary sexuality, God institutes marriage as the context in which a man and a woman are to come together as one flesh. Here is the

---

[20] Croft, *Together in Love and Faith*, 38.
[21] Thomas Schmidt, *Straight and Narrow? Compassion and Clarity in the Homosexuality Debate* (London: IVP, 1995), 44.

basis of the Bible's teaching about what sex is for in God's good design: to bind one man and one woman together in lifelong union and to be the means by which children are to be conceived and raised within that context. Genesis 2:24 is, in effect, the Bible's definition of marriage, which is quoted in the New Testament by both Jesus and Paul: 'A man leaves his father and mother and is united to his wife, and they become one flesh'. All the Bible's negatives concerning alternative contexts for sexual expression, as well as its positive teaching about sexuality, flow from this account of God's creation design. Scripture affirms the goodness of sex within heterosexual marriage and forbids it in every other context.

Bishop Steven acknowledges the importance of Genesis 2:24 when he writes, 'This text (foundational in the traditional understanding of marriage), undoubtedly merits further exploration in the debate around the Church's ability to solemnise a marriage between two people of the same gender'.[22] The lack of any such exploration in his paper is striking, but it does not prevent him from concluding that the verse 'should not prevent the blessing of a same-sex union and partnership', which, he suggests, is 'at the very least... analogous to Christian marriage'.[23] This has the impression of being theology on the hoof – a conclusion waiting for an argument.

---

[22] Croft, *Together in Love and Faith*, 39.

[23] Croft, *Together in Love and Faith*, 39.

Along with Genesis 1 and 2, Genesis 3 is a foundational text. It is important to remember that sin has tainted every aspect of God's good creation, and that we are all corrupted sexually since the Fall, both in desires and behaviour. We cannot trust our instincts and are all, without exception, called to resist behaviour which may well feel very natural to us, as we seek to live for Christ; and, in our different ways, we all fail. There is no place for any judgemental pride in our attitude to others in this or any area of life.

The Bible's chief focus is, of course, not sin, but salvation. The gospel of Christ must be central to all we say on any subject, including sexuality. It is perhaps unfair to criticise Bishop Steven's essay for lacking this emphasis, given how much ground he needed to cover, but I confess that I hungered for more, much more, on this theme. Divorced from the gospel, Christian moral standards become both unattractive and impossible, which is exactly what I thought of them before my conversion. How can we expect the non-Christian world to think anything different? It is only by the Spirit that God's ways become both desirable, because of our longing to please the Saviour we love, and doable, because they are now written on our hearts, rather than on stone tablets.

By writing in this way, I run the risk of underplaying the challenge and cost involved. Yes, it is doable, but that certainly does not make it easy or prevent us from failing. Yet I fear Bishop Steven has fallen in the other direction by giving the impression that it is virtually impossible for a gay/same-sex attracted Christian to live a fulfilled celibate life. All our challenges are insurmountable if we focus on them alone, but life looks very different when seen with the eye of faith. Whatever path we are called to travel as Christians, we do so with our Heavenly Father holding all our concerns within his loving, sovereign care, with our gracious Saviour at our side every step of the way and with the powerful Holy Spirit giving us joy and strength as we travel with him on the road to glory.

Specific texts

Bishop Steven claims that, 'the resistance to changing the current position of the Church of England on sexually active same-sex partnerships is principally focused on the prohibition in biblical texts on sexual activity between two people of the same gender'.[24] This may be true of some conservative arguments but, as I have tried to demonstrate, a responsible handling of the Bible on this subject does not focus on these few verses alone, but rather on the teaching of the sweep of Scripture about sex and marriage. Taken as a whole, these texts conform to what we would expect of that broader teaching, with its affirmation of sex in heterosexual marriage and prohibition of it outside that context.

I agree with the Bishop that the relevant sections of Genesis 19, Deuteronomy 23 and Judges 19 are about rape and prostitution and should therefore not be used as

---

[24] Croft, *Together in Love and Faith*, 30.

the basis for a prohibition of homosexual sex in general. Leviticus 18:22 and 20:13 are, however, broad in scope. It is true that they appear close to other commands, which Christians no longer obey, such as the ban on eating pork or prawns. That might settle the matter for President Bartlett in his tirade against a group of conservative Christians in an episode of *The West Wing*, but a serious engagement with Scripture must go deeper. Jesus came not to abolish the law but to fulfil it (Matthew 5:17). The New Testament makes it clear that what that means in practice varies. Some laws, such as the food laws, no longer apply, as they were intended to mark out the Israelites as distinctive in the old covenant days, which is why Jesus 'declared all foods clean' (Mark 7:19). But moral laws, which are rooted in the character of God and creation principles, still apply and are reaffirmed by Christ and the apostles. It is for this reason that Article 7 of the 39 Articles of the Church of England states: 'No Christian man whatsoever is free from the obedience of the Commandments which are called Moral'.

I write in slightly more detail about the relevant New Testament texts elsewhere.[25] Bishop Steven's arguments as to why they need not be understood as they always have been until very recently are not convincing. 1 Corinthians 6:9–10 and 1 Timothy 1:9–10 are set within a list of behaviours, certainly not limited to sex, which Paul says, if continued and not repented of, will result

---

[25] Vaughan Roberts, *Battles Christians Face* (Milton Keynes: Authentic Media, 2007), 114–116.

in exclusion from the Kingdom of God. They include a word (*arsenekoitai*) which is a composite word, literally meaning 'those that lie with men'. Nothing in the context suggests that it refers only to certain kinds of homosexual behaviour. It should be added that the Apostle would have been well aware of the presence in Gentile culture of the time, not just of male prostitution, or of sex between older men with much younger boys, but also of loving and committed same-sex relationships between adults.

When it comes to Romans 1:26–27, which speaks of both men and women exchanging 'natural sexual relations for unnatural ones', Bishop Steven appears to make no attempt to argue that the Apostle is not saying exactly what he most obviously appears to say: that homosexual behaviour is unnatural, because it goes against God's creation pattern for sex. Instead he says, 'we need to ask the question: Has our understanding of same-sex desire and attraction changed significantly because of advances in science, social science and culture, such that we would now offer a more nuanced interpretation for gender and same gender relations?'.[26] If we were to take that move, it would surely cease to be an interpretation of Romans 1, but rather a nullification of it, in the light of what we are supposed to have learnt from elsewhere. At an earlier point in his argument, he asks 'whether it is possible to adjust and revise the traditional teaching of the Church to accommodate' what he calls 'new and well established

---

[26] Croft, *Together in Love and Faith*, 34.

truths' in relation to human sexuality.[27] What are these 'truths'? Are they really 'well established'? Or are they simply beliefs, such as the view that sexuality is fixed at birth, which are widely accepted by the general public, although it is acknowledged in the essay that 'scientists and doctors continue to debate this'?[28] In this particular clash between the contested 'truth' claims of Scripture and contemporary culture, it appears that the Bishop wants us to preference the latter.

In the essay's treatment of Romans 1, supportive reference is made to a recent article by Walter Brueggemann: 'How to read the Bible on homosexuality', although Bishop Steven does not quote one striking statement it contains concerning the biblical passages we have just been discussing: 'it is impossible to explain away these texts'.[29] This honest admission is in line with the opinion of the vast majority of biblical scholars, of whom Walter Wink is typical: 'Where the Bible mentions homosexual behavior at all, it clearly condemns it. I freely grant that. The issue is precisely whether that biblical judgment is correct'.[30]

---

[27] Croft, *Together in Love and Faith*, 30.

[28] Croft, *Together in Love and Faith*, 19.

[29] Walter Brueggemann, 'How to read the Bible on homosexuality', https://outreach.faith/2022/09/walter-brueggemann-how-to-read-the-bible-on-homosexuality/ (4 Sept 2022).

[30] Walter Wink, 'Homosexuality and the Bible', in Walter Wink (ed.), *Homosexuality and Christian Faith: Questions of Conscience for the Churches* (Minneapolis: Fortress Press, 1999), 47.

The trajectories of Scripture

One final argument Bishop Steven makes in relation to Scripture, using the examples of changing understandings regarding slavery, apartheid and the leadership of women in church, is to say that a change in the Church's position on same-sex partnerships can also be justified on the basis of the overall trajectory of Scripture. The parallels, however, are not persuasive. Only a very small proportion of Christians were persuaded by biblical arguments for apartheid, given the amount of passages which speak so clearly of God's plan for a united church, binding different ethnicities together in Christ. While there are passages which command slaves to obey their masters, others undermine the institution of slavery (e.g. 1 Corinthians 7:21–23 and Philemon). Similarly, alongside passages which appear to place limitations on the ministry of women in churches, others describe them as having prominent roles. However, in relation to homosexual sex, the Bible speaks with complete consistency throughout and there are no passages which even hint at support. The Bishop effectively admits as much by failing to refer to any. He rather appeals to the trajectory he sees in the New Testament 'towards the worth of each individual, the equal value of all humanity, and the freedom which is entrusted to us in Christ'.[31] Those themes are undoubtedly

---

[31] Croft, *Together in Love and Faith*, 35.

strongly affirmed, but they are nowhere understood to trump any clearly expressed moral principle.[32]

If we are to refer to the trajectory of Scripture in relation to its teaching on sex and marriage, we should surely focus above all on the way in which biblical writers in both Old and New Testaments understand human marriage as a metaphor for the relationship of God/Christ and his people. I have written about this great theme in other publications:

> The story of the Bible proclaims the fact that sex and marriage point beyond themselves to something even more wonderful... The Bible begins with human marriage in Genesis 2, but it ends with the marriage of Christ and the Church in Revelation 21 when, at the

---

[32] As for the argument that Bishop Steven makes in relation to Acts 15, there has been much debate about what the apostles meant in their decision at the Council of Jerusalem when they called on Gentile Christians to abstain from certain foods and from 'sexual immorality' (*porneia*), out of sensitivity to their Jewish brothers and sisters. Given that nowhere else in the New Testament is there even a hint that any form of sexual behaviour outside of heterosexual marriage could be in a similar category to Jewish traditional practices, which are in principle matters of freedom, we must surely assume that they did not have this in mind here. One possibility, favoured by many commentators, is that they were referring to the prohibition of marriages to close relatives listed in Leviticus 18.

end of time, Christ and his people will be joined together in perfect intimacy. The former is a trailer of the latter. The marriage of a man and a woman is designed as a picture of a relationship with God, which he offers to us all through Christ. Paul makes this explicit in Ephesians 5:32. Having quoted the Bible's foundational words about human marriage in Genesis 2:24, he adds: 'This is a profound mystery – but I am talking about Christ and the church.'[33]

[The Apostle] is saying that the distinction between men and women reflects the distinction between God and human beings. And the coming together of a man and woman in the deep union of marriage is a reflection of God's desire for us to be united with him – which has now been made possible through Christ. Christ's church – those who trust in him – is his bride (Revelation 21:2). This picture only works because of the difference of the sexes. Two men or two women can't reflect the marriage of Christ and his church. The image

---

[33] Vaughan Roberts, *The Porn Problem* (Epsom: Good Book Company, 2018), 25.

requires the union of two distinct and different, but complementary, "others".[34]

Our sexual longings point even beyond our desire for union with another person. At the deepest level, they bear witness to a spiritual desire for connection with the God who made us in his image to relate to him. That explains why even the best sexual experience and the closest marriage will never completely fulfil us. But one day, when Christ returns, all our longings will be finally and fully satisfied forever.[35]

This teaching is a strong counter to the idolisation of sexual and romantic love, which is so common in our culture. C S Lewis once said that sexual intercourse 'is rapidly becoming the one thing venerated in a world without veneration'.[36] The frequent use of the language of worship in song lyrics supports his claim. The words of Bruno Mars are an especially striking example of a common theme: 'Swimming in your world is something spiritual; I am born again every time you spend the night. Your sex takes me to paradise.'[37] Sadly such sentiments,

[34] Vaughan Roberts, *Transgender* (Epsom: Good Book Company, 2016), 41–42.

[35] Roberts, *The Porn Problem*, 26.

[36] C. S. Lewis, *God in the Dock: Essays on Theology and Ethics*, new edition (Grand Rapids: Eerdmans, 2014), 15.

[37] Bruno Mars, 'Locked out of Heaven' (2012).

although less overtly stated, are also prevalent in many churches, which exalt human marriage as if it is the key to happiness and imply that singleness is a state to be avoided at all costs. This attitude puts pressure both on marriages, which will never be able to live up to the expectations that are raised, and on single people, who can be made to feel that they are missing out on the key to a happy life.

A proper appreciation of the trajectory of the Bible's teaching about marriage encourages us all, whether single or married, to direct our unfulfilled longings above all towards Christ, who alone can fulfil them, in part in this life by the Holy Spirit, and in full in the coming age. While we wait for that consummation, both married and single Christians have an important role to play in pointing to the wonder of the gospel of Christ: marrieds as a reflection of the relationship with Christ and his church, and singles, as witnesses to the sufficiency of Christ for this present age, while we wait for the certain hope of our eternal inheritance in the age to come.

PART TWO:

IS THERE A WAY TO BREAK THE IMPASSE?

What next?

I turn now to consider Bishop Steven's proposals for the way ahead. After various formal processes, culminating with 'Living in Love and Faith', the Church of England is running out of long grass. There is widespread recognition on both sides of the argument that the current situation, with its manifest inconsistencies, is unsustainable. Bishop Steven's paper reflects his determination to move things on and offers a way forward which, he hopes, will break the impasse, while avoiding the damaging splits which have occurred in other provinces of the Anglican Communion, which have already gone down the road of affirming same-sex unions.

There are two elements to what the Bishop is proposing. The first allows clergy and ordinands to have freedom of conscience to order their relationships appropriately, including the right to enter into a same-sex marriage, while also providing for the blessing of same-sex partnerships and the solemnisation of same-sex marriages. The second provides for the protection of the consciences of those who cannot support these changes, including differentiation of provision and oversight of clergy and parishes who would feel the need to distance themselves from those who do.

I need spend little time saying what I disagree with about these proposals, which will be obvious from what has already been written. I could have said much more, for example about the fact that the universal witness of Christian tradition down the ages is against any change to the Church's teaching in this area, which would also put us out of step with the great majority of the worldwide Church today, thus greatly damaging our ecumenical relations. The impact of the mother Church making these changes would also have grave implications for the Anglican Communion, which is already significantly fractured. Along with many others in the Church of England, my prayer is that the House of Bishops will resist calls for change and instead reaffirm and uphold our current teaching and liturgy. If they were to make this reaffirmation, we would still have much work to do in thinking together how to apply this teaching with integrity, grace and sensitivity in our rapidly changing world, in ways which demonstrate loving welcome to all and recognise that sanctification takes time, while not compromising on moral principles. This is an urgent and challenging task, in which wisdom will often require us to resist over-dogmatic or hasty conclusions.

Love and respect

I wholeheartedly agree that any way forward 'must be founded on love and respect' for all, whatever view they take on these contentious issues.[38] I am grateful

---

[38] Croft, *Together in Love and Faith*, 45.

for Bishop Steven's warning against 'reaching for the emotive language of abuse' in relation to those who hold a conservative position and for his affirmation of their ministry 'often including the welcome and care extended to LGBTQ+ people'.[39] I am sorry for times when those advocating a conservative position have used inappropriate language themselves and have attacked a person or people, rather than critiqued a position. Caricatures and demonisation have no place in Christ's church from either side of these divisions. Once again, I pay tribute to Bishop Steven for his own gracious example.

A fudge is untenable

Despite my initial scepticism about the Living in Love and Faith process, I acknowledge that it has achieved much of value. Most of those involved speak of the benefit they have received from getting to know, listening to and learning from those who bring a variety of perspectives and experiences to issues of sexuality. I have heard of few, however, who have come to a radically different view as a result. We understand each other better, but we remain deeply divided. Far from finding one another somewhere in the middle, if anything in recent years we have polarised more into two distinct and irreconcilable positions, both of which are held with integrity, passion and deep Christian conviction. This reality has become evident in the last General Synod elections, which

---

[39] Croft, *Together in Love and Faith*, 46.

resulted in large blocs on both sides, with only a few floating voters in the middle.

Not long ago some had hoped, including it seems Bishop Steven, that a way forward could be found that would gain support from the majority on both sides: the allowance for clergy in parishes who wish to bless gay unions to do so, while not making any formal changes to the liturgy and doctrine of the Church. It has become clear that this is untenable. Many liberals would now find this to be insultingly inadequate and many conservatives would regard it as a step too far, because we believe it would involve a de facto change in the Church's doctrine. Any move of this kind, or something equivalent, would not settle anything, but rather simply increase the divisions and turmoil that already exist. This is a depressing prospect. There is a terrible cost to these internal arguments in the time and energy they occupy, the damage they cause to our mission and in the emotional impact they have, especially on those most intimately engaged in the issues, above all, those of us who are gay/same-sex attracted. Any attempted fudge will only prolong and intensify the agony.

Differentiation is necessary

There is nothing radical or surprising about Bishop Steven's proposal that any change in the Church's theology and practice would also need to ensure the protection of the consciences of those who could not support it. A lack of such provision would surely be unthinkable at least in the short term. He does, however, go significantly further than this in also proposing 'a differentiation of ministry and oversight'.[40] This is a big concession for a bishop to make and is a position he admits he came to gradually, after extended dialogue with conservatives.

From my own conversations with those who take a different position to me, it is clear that many have not come to understand, as Bishop Steven has, why it is that many conservatives feel such significant differentiation would be needed if the Church was to make any change in its position. There are two reasons behind this conviction: pastoral and theological.

Perhaps the pastoral reason can be introduced if I speak personally. When Bishop Steven was first open about his change of view regarding same-sex unions, he stressed that he wanted to pastor all his clergy, whatever their views on the matter. I found myself instinctively blurting out, perhaps too forcefully, 'but you can't pastor me!' I did not mean it personally. I like, honour, and respect Bishop Steven, and have always known that he wants the best for me, but the fact that he takes such a different view from me on an issue that causes such conflict and heartache in my life in the world, the Church and internally, means that it is very difficult for me to imagine turning to him as my pastor. I can understand why someone in a same-sex partnership might feel the same way about being pastored by me. It is hard to see how we can change our

---

[40] Croft, *Together in Love and Faith*, 46.

practice and still maintain normal ecclesial relations, with no differentiation, without causing significant distress to those on both sides of the argument. It is impossible to bless people in same-sex partnerships and also, at the same time, affirm and encourage those gay/ same-sex attracted Christians who feel in principle they must remain celibate. We will not be able to pastor both sensitively without pastoral differentiation.

There are also theological reasons behind the necessity of differentiation. The importance of Christian unity is strongly emphasised in the New Testament. At times, when second order issues are involved, the apostles stress the importance of freedom of conscience, which should be exercised with love, so as to hold those with different convictions together; but there are other more fundamental matters over which it is not permissible simply to agree to disagree. Whereas most evangelicals regard disagreements over women priests and bishops as belonging to the first category, they are clear, because of the apostles' teaching, that differences over the issues we are discussing belong to the second. Although in 1 Corinthians 7–8 Paul speaks of disagreements over circumcision or food sacrificed to idols as matters that should not divide the church, in chapter 5 he insists that church discipline must be exercised where there is ongoing sexual sin with no repentance. In chapter 6 he mentions sexual immorality, including homosexual activity, among behaviours that, if persisted in, prevent people from inheriting the Kingdom of God. The Lord

Jesus condemned the Christians in Thyatira because they 'tolerate' a woman whose teaching is seducing people to practise sexual immorality (Revelation 2:20). Elsewhere the apostles call on Christians not to give a platform to those who teach error (Titus 1:11) and to keep their distance from them (2 John 7–11).

Already these principles have caused a few faithful Christians to leave the Church of England and others to create distance between themselves and their bishops. It is for this reason that we at St Ebbe's have asked for bishops other than our diocesan or area bishops for Ministerial Development Reviews, Confirmations and Ordinations (and Bishop Steven has graciously agreed). Many would feel the need for much more radical differentiation if the Church's official position was to change. If any believe that the numbers involved would be small, they should learn from what has happened in other provinces of the Anglican Communion, which have already acted to bless same-sex unions.

Some seem to have the naive belief that, in the event of revisionist change, almost all clergy in parishes would accept it, without the need for any radical disruption, even if they personally did not participate. A look across the Atlantic at The Episcopal Church in America should make us think again. In the last few years, as they have made moves to bless gay unions, they have lost 100,000 members, many hundreds of clergy have left or been deposed, and vast sums have been spent in litigation over the ownership of buildings. The cost, of course, has been far more than just financial, and has had an horrific emotional, spiritual and missional impact. I have long feared that we are sleep-walking towards a similar disaster here. We need to learn from the experience of other provinces in the Communion (which is the focus of the video from the Church of England Evangelical Council (CEEC) 'Learning from Elsewhere'[41]) and urgently seek to find a better way.

A better way?

Bishop Steven recognises that 'some alternative system of episcopal oversight may well be required to enable a differentiation of ministries, such as an alternative province and structure within the Church of England or a system of oversight from a neighbouring diocese'.[42] No doubt the immediate reaction to such proposals will be cautious and often negative. I have witnessed similar reactions from many on both sides of these discussions. The instinctive reaction has tended to be that such provision is either unnecessary, unachievable, or both. I have argued already why some such differentiation is necessary, but I do not want to underestimate how hard it will be to deliver, given the significant disruption it would involve. But what are the alternatives?

Like Bishop Steven, I have been involved in informal dialogues in recent years with those who have held

---

[41] This can be found on the CEEC website (www.ceec.info) along with other relevant videos in the *God's Beautiful Story* series.
[42] Croft, *Together in Love and Faith*, 47.

different convictions about same-sex partnerships. Having recognised from the beginning that we were very unlikely to change each other's minds, we were able to focus on discussing how we can move forward as a Church, given the fact of our irreconcilable differences. As time has moved on, we have experienced a growing convergence on certain matters. Almost without exception, we have agreed that the present position is untenable, a fudge will not work and that, without creative thinking and much prayer, our current wranglings will continue exhaustingly long into the future, with much damage caused along the way.

The winner takes all approach of other provinces is unlikely to work here, given the strength on both sides, but if it could be achieved, it would cause an even more painful and destructive division. All this has made us ask with greater urgency whether it might be possible to find some kind of settlement which would break the impasse and allow both groups to move forward with their integrity intact. There is undoubtedly a long way to go, but these private discussions have given me hope that what is too quickly dismissed by many as a pipe dream might just be possible. We certainly differ on what would be necessary. My conviction is that it would need to be of a provincial nature and, not surprisingly, my strong preference would be for the creation of a new distinct province for those who wish for a change in the Church's teaching and practice. Others, of course, have a different solution in mind. None of the options will be entirely satisfactory to everyone and ground will need to be given by all, without abandoning core convictions. The aim should be settlement without compromise.

Although I have shown my strong disagreement with much in Bishop Steven's essay, I am nonetheless hopeful that it might help somehow to move us forward in our discussions within the Church of England. The deep disagreements it exposes reveal the depth of our theological differences and the reality that we will not be able simply to agree to disagree. That in itself demonstrates the necessity of a more radical approach to how we handle these differences as we move forward. More importantly, the essay points us towards a way that might just enable us to do that, as well as modelling a spirit that will be necessary for many of us to adopt if we are to have any chance of success. May God have mercy on us and guide us in the ways of truth and love in the days ahead.

Other Recommendations

In the Christian Leadership series

Bishops Past, Present and Future: A Concise Study summarises the key points of the argument of Martin's major study *Bishops Past, Present and Future* (Gilead Books, 2022). It is designed to meet the needs of those who would like to know about the role and importance of bishops in the Church of England, but who would baulk at tackling the 800+ pages of the original book.

This concise study is published in the hope that it will help many in the Church of England, both ordained and lay, to think in a more informed fashion about how bishops should respond to the challenges facing the Church of England at this critical point in its history as it considers how to move forward following the publication of the Living in Love and Faith material.

In the St Antholin Lectures series

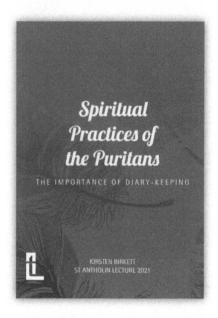

The Puritans wished to live godly lives in heart and thought as well as action. One of the tools they utilised in training their hearts and minds was the practice of diary-writing. In this short overview we see the theory of Puritan diary-writing as worked out by John Beadle, and the inspiring example of the sixteenth-century Puritan Richard Rogers writing about his life.

Also published by the Latimer Trust

Prepared for the Renew Conference

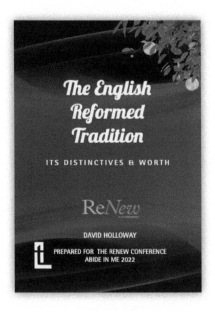

The Reformation in Europe produced different traditions according to the influential people and theological climate of each country. But what is it that makes the English Reformed tradition as expressed in the Church of England? This short booklet, produced for Renew, considers the Anglican distinctives as compared with other Reformed traditions, and the enduring importance of preserving this rich heritage.

Lightning Source UK Ltd.
Milton Keynes UK
UKHW011952151122
412254UK00005B/402

9 781906 327781